D0354463

People Who Have Helped the World

FLORENCE NIGHTINGALE
by Pam Brown

Picture Credits

J. Bethell, p. 11 (below); Bridgeman Art Library, pp. 12, 24, 50; Forbes Collection, pp. 13, 33 (above); Giraudon, p. 17; Royal Holloway College, p. 54; Victoria & Albert Museum, p. 33 (below); City Art Gallery, Manchester, p. 31; Mary Evans Picture Library, p. 34; Fine Art Photographic Library, p. 4; Fotomas Index, cover, pp. 23, 24 (below), 44 (below); GLC Photo Library, pp. 9, 10, 35, 36, 41 (left), 46, 57 (top), 59; Illustrated London News, pp. 11, 28, 32, 38, 52; Mansell Collection, pp. 14, 15, 18, 29, 44 (left); National Army Museum, pp. 40 (top), 42; National Portrait Gallery, pp. 8, 16, 43; National Trust, pp. 8, 57 (below, both); Royal Collections, reproduced by gracious permission of Her Majesty the Queen, p. 30; Royal College of Nursing, p. 41 (right); George Weidenfeld & Nicholson Ltd., p. 20; Welcome Medical Museum, p. 40 (below); Zefa Picture Library, p. 48.

Maps drawn by Geoffrey Pleasance

North American edition first published in 1989 by
Gareth Stevens, Inc.
7317 West Green Tree Road
Milwaukee, WI 53223 USA

First published in the United Kingdom in 1989 with an original text
© 1989 by Exley Publications Ltd.
Additional end matter © 1989 by Gareth Stevens, Inc.

Library of Congress Cataloging-in-Publication Data

Brown, Pam, 1928-
   Florence Nightingale.

   (People who have helped the world)
   Includes index.
   1. Nightingale, Florence, 1820-1910. 2. Nurses--England--Biography. I. Title. II. Series.
RT37.N5B76   1988   610.73'092'4 [B]   88-4913
ISBN 1-55532-885-7
ISBN 1-55532-860-1 (lib. bdg.)

Series conceived and edited by Helen Exley
Picture research: Kate Duffy
Research: Diana Briscoe
Series editor, U.S.: Rhoda Irene Sherwood
Editorial assistant, U.S.: Scott Enk
Additional end matter, U.S.: Ric Hawthorne

Printed in Hungary

1 2 3 4 5 6 7 8 9 94 93 92 91 90 89

FLORENCE NIGHTINGALE

*The determined Englishwoman
who founded modern nursing
and reformed military medicine*

by Pam Brown

Gareth Stevens Publishing
Milwaukee

The Nightingales abroad

The great coach lurched as the six sweating horses reached the top of the pass, but these Italian roads were nothing compared to the rough ones in France. Papa barely looked up from his book of Greek verse. Mama, half asleep, stirred drowsily but without alarm. Florence stared out into the gathering dusk. Beside her was her devoted but oftentimes quite jealous sister, Parthenope.

It was February 1838, and the Nightingale family was touring Europe. The carriage was roomy enough inside to accommodate nine or ten people and had many then-new conveniences to add to the passengers' comfort. The servants sat on the roof. Whenever the views were spectacular and the weather nice, Florence and her sister joined them on top.

The carriage might have been large and comfortable, but horrible roads and flea-ridden inns meant that such journeys were still a great adventure requiring both stamina and courage. The Nightingales had enjoyed themselves hugely, especially Florence, whose diary was bursting with all the excitement that she had experienced since leaving England the previous September. It had all been such a wonderful contrast to life at home — "like an Arabian Nights dream come true," she wrote.

Despite the busy life that the family had in England, caught up in the activities of innumerable cousins and aunts and uncles, Florence found her existence there wearisome. At eighteen she was pretty and clever — more so than Parthenope — but Florence was a strange mixture of clearheadedness and oversensitivity. She began to retreat into fantasies she knew might take over her whole life.

Parthenope, or Parthe as she was known, was a year older than Florence and far more like their

An early photograph of Florence. She was shy, modest, and kind. But during the years of family conflict, she developed a steely determination that would help her in the years of campaign ahead.

Opposite: Nightingale was born into a wealthy family and would not have been expected to work for a living. The whole family could afford to travel around Europe for seven months at a time with their own carriage and six servants. Their coach was grander than the one in this picture. It held eleven people, with all their luggage, and was drawn by six horses.
(Painting by Heywood Hardy)

outgoing mother, Fanny Smith Nightingale, than their studious father, William Edward Nightingale. She did not enjoy the long hours of lessons in Greek, Latin, German, French, history, and philosophy that he imposed. And she may have been envious because Florence excelled in every subject.

The past December they had reached Nice, on the southern coast of France. Many English people lived there, and Florence was swept away in a passion for balls and dancing. When they got to Genoa, a city on Italy's coast, she found that there were even more balls, more concerts and operas, more splendid sights to see — and more very friendly grand dukes and other young men to admire the two sisters, especially Florence. She was "much noticed." The next stop was the Italian city of Florence, where she had been born on May 12, 1820.

The city that shared her name proved to be more exciting than she had hoped. The past seemed as alive as the present. There were magnificent palaces, churches, paintings, and statues everywhere — and they seemed almost as alive as the well-dressed people who came from all over the world to admire them. And there was music. The city was alive with opera and dance — and Nightingale became "music-mad."

In the city of Florence, a young woman named Florence was caught up in a whirl of music and gaiety. She often danced all night. For her, the winter of 1838 went by in a flurry of dances and operas — a swirl of silks and lace, concerts and music. With spring came outdoor parties and dancing under the trees.

A woman of two minds

After a summer tour of Italy's beautiful lakes, the family moved on to Geneva in Switzerland. That September, the city was full of people fleeing Austrian tyranny. Florence began to learn about a world totally different from hers. It was one of poverty, hardship, courage, and determination.

She had always been a person of two minds. Part of her mind was quite disciplined, but another part was passionate. This would always prove to be a source of inner conflict for her, especially now that she fought

Parthenope and Florence. Demure and proper young ladies of breeding filled their time before marriage with reading, music, embroidery, and perhaps with a discreet visit to some deserving poor family on the estate. Nightingale wanted more for herself. She rejected a way of life that she thought would not finally make her happy.

fantasies and longed for the challenge of hard reality.

She loved the excitement of her social world, but another part of her demanded order. Her diaries were full of enthusiasm, but they were carefully kept, listing facts about everything that caught her interest.

Between her notes on receptions, dances, sights, and paintings were notes about the plight of the poor. The fun had not blinded her to the misery of people living in areas touched by war. She had been taken to Europe to learn and she had — but she had learned about more than merely dancing, music, paintings, and architecture.

Through all the months of travel, Florence had had a secret that would eventually shape her entire life.

In a private note, she wrote about something that she said happened to her on February 7, 1837 — months before she left for Europe. "God," she wrote,

"spoke to me and called me to His service." From that day on, Nightingale was convinced that one day this "call" would be clear to her and when it was, she must obey, however hard the task turned out to be. She was sure that she had a special mission. But sixteen years were to pass between her first call and the day she could serve others as she felt God wanted her to.

The shadow of home

When Florence returned to England in 1839, her life, at least outwardly, did not seem to change. Family members divided their time between their two country homes and London. Her parents were unaware of her desire to serve others and her growing lack of interest in the conventional life of a well-to-do young Englishwoman in the middle of the nineteenth century.

Anyone who met Nightingale was struck by her vivid good looks, her grace, and her wit. Intelligent as she was beautiful, she was full of life. Many admired her. She became caught up in a summer of laughter and dancing. Henry Nicholson, the brother of her cousin and best friend, Marianne, fell in love with her, but she did not love him. Florence's mother, Fanny, had great hopes for her — a brilliant marriage, a country estate, and a house in London, perhaps even success as a great hostess.

By this time, Florence had put her call out of her mind, but as the year went on, the memory of it began to haunt her.

A rare, early photograph of Florence Nightingale. When she escaped from her family, she dressed more simply, turning her back on the fashionable society of her childhood.

Young, wealthy, and cultured women of her time were expected to be well-mannered, respectably religious, and busy with small concerns. In wealthy families like hers, servants did the work, and the men of the house pursued their professions. There was little or no hope of a woman's taking up any real career.

But many of these same wealthy people saw nothing wrong with the idea that working-class women should slave away in hot, noisy, and dangerous factories from dawn to dusk, that these women should be employed in terrible, backbreaking work, or even that they should be forced into prostitution because sewing for the rich paid too little to live on.

Meanwhile, women like Florence often suffered too, but in a different way. Their lives were boring. Most men were nervous about a woman with opinions, much less ambitions. A handful of women succeeded in "feminine" fields like writing or painting, but even they often had great difficulties to overcome. "Ladies" were supposed to marry well, raise families, and be submissive and supportive wives.

But Florence was an educated, concerned human being. She was suffocating among the teacups and potted ferns, the polite conversations, and the endless evenings sitting around the fire when there were no invitations to dine or dance. She felt like screaming. Instead, she bit her tongue — and became more depressed. The inner conflict between her desires and what her society expected of her might well have made her physically ill. The family sent her off to stay with her Aunt Mai in London. They felt more socializing, not less, would cure Florence's gloom.

When Florence got to London, Britain's new, young ruler, Queen Victoria, was about to marry her adored Albert. Florence was caught up in the nation's excitement. She appeared to be much better. No one could sense her growing unhappiness. But she felt she was filling her days with silly, useless things. Part of her could still get pleasure from them, but an inner feeling that she was only wasting her time and her life gnawed at her. What was she to do about her call?

While Florence longed for useful work, the vast majority of women lived in poverty, working long, hard hours for a pittance of a wage.

Mathematics

Desperate for something challenging to do, she took up the study of mathematics. It gave her weary, confused mind something to focus on, something clear, precise, and disciplined. Aunt Mai understood her need. "Florence and I have been getting up at 6, lighting our fire and sitting very comfortably at our work," she wrote to Florence's mother. "I think if she had a subject which required *all* her powers and which she pursued regularly and vigorously for a couple of hours she would be happier all day for it."

But Florence's mother did not approve. Florence's destiny, in her opinion, was to marry well and become a respectable wife and mother. What use was mathematics? Even Florence's intellectual father thought history or philosophy would be more sensible.

Florence was developing the stubborn streak that was to be her salvation. She stuck to mathematics.

Soon, however, she returned home, where no one

Fanny Nightingale, Florence's mother. Unlike Florence, she enjoyed the social nights and idle days of the British upper classes.

Many religious people of the time believed that God had decided how each individual should live. The rich believed that God had approved of their wealth and success and had, in his wisdom, created the lower classes to do all the disagreeable work in life. Those with a conscience saw that the poor were kept from actual starvation. The contrasts between the two classes could be striking.

encouraged her interest in math. She grew more and more miserable. She struggled to continue her studies on her own. Up in her bedroom, she studied alone, working in the cold, early hours before the rest of the household was awake.

She felt she was drowning, her time consumed by countless small tasks. Because she was only twenty-two and unmarried, she was at everyone's beck and call. It was her duty to make herself "useful." She was always busy with family and social activities, but it seemed pointless.

Waking up

Nightingale lived at a time when England seemed to be divided into two nations, rich and poor.

Unlike many well-off people of her time, Nightingale began to see the misery and injustice. When she went to dinner at the homes of wealthy friends, she saw that their dinner tables were weighed down with food! She looked at the wealthy classes, many of whom were frittering away their lives and wearing

expensive clothes sewn by starving girls who worked day and night for starvation wages.

She wrote: "My mind is absorbed with the idea of the sufferings of man. . . . I can hardly see anything else. All the people I see are eaten up with care or poverty or disease." She now knew her mission was to help the unfortunate, but how? She ached to be useful, but what could she do?

Finding a mission

Then, at the age of twenty-four, she suddenly saw exactly what she could do. She could work in hospitals among the sick. Today, most people would call this a sensible and praiseworthy goal. But in 1844, this idea was considered impossible.

Hospitals were then places to be afraid of. People avoided entering them. They were dark, poorly run, and dirty. Patients with all sorts of different diseases were crammed into the same ward, even the same bed. It was not uncommon to see a man with a broken leg sharing his mattress with another patient who was

This oil painting shows Florence's social background. The men ran everything. Florence would be expected to look pretty and arrange flowers or sing. She couldn't even take an interest in cooking, because that was servants' work. Florence was one of the first women to break this rigid mold. She said no to marriage and as a result suffered greatly from the break with her family and with society. She paid a high personal price in order to have her own life.
(Painting by George Smith)

A cartoon of a sleeping, drunken nurse. Nurses were regarded as lazy and disreputable, so we can understand why Florence's family was alarmed by the idea of her working in hospitals.

"There was usually but one 'nurse' to a ward who swept, dusted, laid the fire, sifted the ashes, fetched the coal, worked from six in the morning until six at night and had no regular holiday. After the manual labour was done she could care for the sick. Patients able to tip the nurse received, not unnaturally, first attention when the dressings needed changing. Those too poor to tip had to wait for days and died in waiting."

Elizabeth Burton, from The Early Victorians at Home

dying of tuberculosis. The concept of hygiene was barely understood. The wooden floors of some hospitals were never scrubbed, and the damp, dirty walls were covered with dirt and fungi. Patients' friends and relatives would smuggle gin and brandy into the hospitals. Beds were often soaked with urine, and the bedding was often not changed for any new patient. People who walked into hospitals often became nauseated by the sights and the stench.

Doctors did not wash their hands before surgery. They wore their street clothes into the operating room, protecting them from splattered blood with the same grimy coat worn to previous operations.

Far from being angels of mercy, nurses had a reputation for being drunken, careless, and dirty. People looked down on nurses — only the very worst women worked in the squalor of hospitals! No respectable woman could possibly tolerate the sights and sounds of such places. So Nightingale could not even mention her newly found mission to her family.

A first step

During the summer of 1844, an American philanthropist, Dr. Samuel Howe, came to stay with the Nightingales. Nightingale asked him for advice — would it not be possible for a respectable woman to be a nurse? It would be difficult, he said, but "it would be a very good thing." He encouraged her. A year went by, and Florence still did not know how to break into nursing. She knew she must have training. In 1845 she decided to go to an infirmary for three months to learn nursing.

Her mother was horrified and disgusted at the idea. Parthe was shocked. It was out of the question.

Florence begins to fight

Eight years had passed since she'd first felt that God had called her to serve others. "I went down into the depths," she wrote in her diary.

Despite pressure from her friends and family, she had refused a proposal of marriage from Henry Nicholson. She was determined now to follow her vocation. Secretly she began to study hospital reports

The Nurse — Old Style

— anything she could find that would tell her about the way they were run and what was needed for their improvement. Long before dawn, she would be at her desk, writing — begging friends for reports on German and French hospitals — for every scrap of information she could gather.

Every morning, she smoothed her hair, put aside her papers, and went downstairs to live the dull, monotonous life of the daughter of a well-to-do household. To the outside world, Florence Nightingale did not seem at all unusual. No one suspected her hidden life of study.

Then, in October 1846, when she was twenty-six, a friend sent her information about an Institution of Deaconesses — women much like nuns — at Kaiserswerth, Germany. It was a place where respectable, religious women nursed the sick. For Nightingale, Kaiserswerth was a flicker of hope in the darkness. Surely her mother could not object to her going to a well-known place with such a good reputation.

But she couldn't mention it yet. Finally, the strain of both keeping up her hard, secret course of study and fighting her unhappiness was making her ill.

From the first day she walked into a hospital, Florence realized that the key to changing the hospital system was to make sure that nursing became reputable. In her lifetime, she transformed nursing into one of the most respected of all professions. She later wrote, "If a patient is cold, if a patient is feverish, if a patient is faint, if he is sick after taking food, if he has a bed sore, it is generally the fault not of the disease, but of the nursing."

Sidney Herbert. For many years, he was Florence's loyal friend. As England's Secretary at War, he would invite her to go out to organize nurses for the Crimean War. He literally worked himself into the grave in supporting Nightingale's cause.

Return to Rome

Near the end of 1847, when Nightingale was twenty-seven, she had a nervous breakdown. Two worried friends, Charles and Selina Bracebridge, whisked her away to Rome in the hope that the change would do her good. The six months Nightingale spent there gave her back her health. They also gave her the friendship of Sidney Herbert, a man who would be more important to her than any other — not because they would become involved romantically, but because they would do great work together.

When she returned to London, refreshed from her trip, Florence worked in some happy, well-run orphanages. As always, she made careful, thoughtful notes of what she saw and learned.

But she still felt frustrated. Rome had been glorious, but it had solved none of her problems. Her mother and sister still could not see why she did not accept and like their own way of life.

No to marriage

By 1849 she was depressed again; she feared she was going insane. She had not wanted to marry Henry Nicholson, so it had been no real hardship to refuse him. But now she was in love with another man, Richard Monckton Milnes, whom she'd known for seven years. An intelligent, talented poet and philanthropist, he became to Florence "the man I adored."

But now Nightingale knew that marriage would not be for her. It would prevent her from being of service and following her call.

After a great deal of hard, painful thought, she refused Milnes' offer of marriage. It nearly broke her heart. Her mother was furious.

She decided to visit Egypt and Greece with friends and tried to take an educated interest in all she saw. She took notes and she read deeply, but it still seemed as if only one part of her mind enjoyed the trip.

But her torment in Egypt gave her new determination. On July 31, 1850, she finally got to visit Kaiserswerth in Germany. The village pastor there had realized while traveling around Europe that Kaiserswerth needed better nurses. He had opened a local hospital with committed, caring deaconesses nursing the sick. Here, Nightingale saw that nursing could be respectable — and worthwhile. She stayed for two weeks, watching how the nurses worked and helping with the children there. She left feeling "so brave as if nothing could ever vex me again."

It had been a short stay, but what she saw inspired her to write a pamphlet on the work of the nurses there. She wanted to persuade other privileged women like herself to take up similar work, instead of wasting their days and minds on tea parties and carriage drives.

She reached home on August 21, 1850, with her heart high. Safe in her pocket was Athena, a pet owl she had rescued from some boys at the Parthenon in Athens, Greece.

She was met by bitter disapproval. Her mother and sister were hostile. Parthe became hysterical. Her mother stormed at her, telling her she had disgraced the family and must never mention Kaiserswerth again. Perhaps she realized that, despite all her efforts, Florence was escaping her and was not going to be the sort of daughter she wanted and expected her to be.

The Doctor for the Poor, a contemporary painting by J. Leonard. Bad housing and long factory hours meant serious health problems for city people. It was work by men like this doctor that inspired Florence to spend her life helping the poor.

Six months with Parthe

Nightingale was now thirty but no nearer her goal than when she had first heard her call at sixteen, more than thirteen years before. All she wanted was her parents' permission to return to Kaiserswerth.

Today, not many grown women would even think of asking their parents' approval of their plans. But Florence was living in 1850, not 1950 or 1990. In a middle-class Victorian home, unmarried daughters were as much under their parents' control as they were when small children.

Now things became worse for Nightingale. Parthe became more hysterical and ill. Florence's parents told her that she was heartless and unfeeling to her devoted sister. She had had a year on her own away from home, while Parthe had had nothing. Her parents insisted that she make up for her year of "selfish" freedom by doing nothing but taking care of Parthe for the next six months. Nightingale, once again, gave in.

When her six months were over, Nightingale went immediately to stay with Sidney Herbert's wife, Liz. The Herberts, sympathetic to her desire to break away from home, encouraged her in her ambition to become a doctor. Florence spent time with Dr. Elizabeth Blackwell, the first woman to get a medical degree in the United States. From Dr. Blackwell, Nightingale learned that a woman could achieve great things. She realized she had to take decisive action if she were to accomplish her own mission.

First she accepted the fact that her family would never support her in her ambition. "I must expect no sympathy or help from them," she wrote in June 1851. "I have so long craved for their sympathy that I can hardly reconcile myself to this. . . . I have been so long treated as a child, and have so long allowed myself to be treated as a child."

Two weeks after she wrote this, she had arranged to return to Kaiserswerth. Her parents forbade her to tell anyone exactly where she was going and why. But they could no longer stop her. Her mother and sister went with her to Germany, pretending that they were taking Florence with them for a three-month stay at the spa at Carlsbad, in what is now Czechoslovakia.

Whenever she could, Florence would secretly visit hospitals. It was quite common to see two people in one bed. Patients with all kinds of diseases were crowded into dirty, disorganized wards. The smell was often so offensive that the hospitals had to be sprayed with perfume. Doctors would make their rounds with handkerchiefs over their noses. Florence Nightingale would later write, pointedly, "The first requirement of a hospital is that it should do the sick no harm."

Back to Kaiserswerth

Life at Kaiserswerth was hard. The students rose at 5:00 A.M. The food provided for the women was simple and sparse. Meals lasted only ten minutes. The days were filled with frequent moments of prayer. All the people in a room would get down on their knees and offer themselves to God.

But despite these hardships, Nightingale was happier than she had ever been in her life. She had escaped the life of boredom led by most well-bred English society women. At the age of thirty-one, she was finally performing some of the tasks she had longed to perform for many years. She was finally leading a life filled with worthwhile work.

Full of a sense of confidence and purpose in life, Nightingale wrote one last pleading letter to her family. "Give me time, give me faith," she asked. "Trust me, help me. . . . Give me your blessing." Her mother and sister made no reply. Nightingale was never to ask for their help or understanding again.

Cassandra

Nightingale returned from Kaiserswerth along with her mother and sister. She was full of plans to plunge into the study of nursing at a large London teaching hospital. But back home, she found her father in severe pain with an eye ailment. He needed Florence to look after him, and she felt she could not refuse. She had to go with her father on a trip so that he could receive special treatment. In a way this journey proved to be a turning point. By the time she and her father returned home, Florence had persuaded him to become an ally in her struggle against Parthe and her mother. He would often intervene to help Florence.

During this period, Nightingale wrote an essay called *Cassandra*. In it, she describes with great bitterness a typical day in the life of a young woman born into a prosperous Victorian family. "We can never pursue any object for a single two hours, for we can never command any . . . solitude," she complained. "And in social and domestic life one is bound, under pain of being thought sulky, to make a remark every two minutes."

"The late age of marriage, low marriage rates, wars and migration had created a pool of spinster labour. The single woman was prevented by powerful social pressures from competing in almost any field against the dominant male sex. If she did not marry, she must either remain at home to do the flowers, help her mother arrange tea-parties, or carry broth and jelly to the sick poor."

Madeleine Masson, from A Pictorial History of Nursing

"What is my business in this world and what have I done this fortnight? I have read Daughter at Home *to father and two chapters of Mackintosh, a volume of Sybil to Mamma. Learnt seven tunes by heart. Written various letters. Ridden with Papa. Paid eight visits. Done company. And that is all."*

Florence Nightingale, from her notebook, 1846

Trapped again

Trapped by her family once more, the desperate Nightingale, a devout Protestant, asked a head of the Roman Catholic Church in England, Archdeacon Henry Edward Manning, for advice. Manning, who later became a cardinal, worked with the poor of London's East End. He suggested that even though she was a Protestant, her best hopes for nursing training were at Catholic hospitals run by the Sisters of Mercy in Dublin, Ireland, or the Sisters of Charity in Paris. Florence began to consider these ideas.

England was a place of passionate religious loyalties. When Florence's mother and sister heard of Nightingale's ideas, they flew into a rage that was more violent than any before.

Parthe was so upset that she was taken to see the queen's physician, Sir James Clark. In August 1852, he arranged for Parthe to go to his home in Scotland, where she could be observed for several weeks. Dr. Clark soon reached a conclusion. He summoned Nightingale from Dublin and told her that she must leave so that Parthe could learn to live on her own, without Nightingale. Nightingale, in short, would have to leave home for the good of her sister.

Finding freedom

Nightingale had never realized before that every time she gave in to Parthe, she was only making her sister feel worse. Now, with Dr. Clark's advice, she saw that it was better if she ignored Parthe's complaints and pleas as much as possible and got on with her own life.

She decided to go to Paris, where she planned to stay at the hospital of the Catholic Sisters of Charity, dressing as a nun but living separately from the sisters.

She arrived in Paris in February 1853.

All her pent-up energies came into action. She visited hospitals, infirmaries, almshouses, and other institutions. She watched Paris's famous surgeons at work. She walked the wards with doctors and watched them examine patients with every kind of disease.

She circulated a questionnaire to French, German, and English hospitals, comparing their answers and making notes, charts, and lists. The knowledge that she had gained during her years of secret study was of use at last. Her natural gifts for order, research, and decision making were finally being used to the fullest. She had become an expert in her field.

Nightingale's first job

In 1853 she sought and accepted the post of Superintendent at London's Institution for the Care of Sick Gentlewomen in Distressed Circumstances. She was to reorganize the institution completely. It was agreed that she would start her new job as soon as the institution could find a new location. For the first time, she would have a professional post where she could do the work she had prepared for her whole life. It was sixteen years after her call to serve God and humanity.

The news of this job aroused new anger in Florence's mother and Parthe. They wept, reproached Florence, refused to eat, and took to their beds. Florence ignored her mother and sister. Florence's father moved out. But now his daughter's ally, he decided to help Florence by making her financially independent. His wife was furious. Nightingale moved into her own rooms in London. Her family objected, but she refused to give in. She was her own woman at last.

At 1 Upper Harley Street

At the age of thirty-three, Florence Nightingale began to live her true calling. On August 12, 1853, she moved into the institution's new quarters at 1 Upper Harley Street, London.

At once, it seem as if her lost years suddenly burst into flower. Nightingale threw herself into the countless tasks involved in organizing the hospital. She had just ten days to equip an empty house and make it ready for patients to move into.

Florence was everywhere, exploring and making requests for new equipment. Soon hot water was piped to every floor. Elevators were put in to carry food up from the kitchens. A system of bells was installed, so that the patients could call the nurse on their floor.

The hospital directors and committee and staff members were astounded. They had expected changes

"The nurses did not as a general rule wash patients, they could never wash their feet — and it was with difficulty and only in great haste that they could have a drop of water just to dab their hands and face. The beds on which the patients lay were dirty. It was common practice to put a patient into the same sheets used by the last occupant of the bed, and mattresses were generally of flock, sodden, and seldom, if ever, cleaned."

Florence Nightingale on a visit to a hospital, 1845

— but nothing like this! Nightingale was years ahead of most people in these matters — and her long endurance had taught her not to take "no" for an answer.

The committee began to wonder if it had made a wise choice in Nightingale. Nightingale quietly steam-rollered members into submission. She had the facts. She had the figures. It could be done. It must be done. Released from the chains of Victorian family life, she was proving to be a formidable person. She never had vague ideas for improvements. She knew exactly how everything should work, how the bell system should function, how much coal was needed. She checked the pantries. She checked the linen closets.

Straight to the top

Nothing was too minor for her attention. Out went ragged, filthy bedsheets, out went soiled and stinking armchairs, out went rotted pillows. She even acquired old curtains and had them made into new bedspreads. She bought new brooms, brushes, and dusters — and saw to it that they were used often. She found that the hospital could make its own jam for the patients much more cheaply then it could buy it on the outside.

The committee reeled at her changes. So did the staff. Many were fired or quit of their own accord. Nightingale hired a more efficient and hard-working housekeeper. But her main problem was finding properly trained nurses.

It was exhausting work. She had to make hard, unpopular decisions, often against great opposition, but she was wonderfully, remarkably happy.

Some committee members and staff members might have disliked her, but patients and poor people admired her. She rubbed the feet of patients if she found them cold, and she did her best to help women who were without hope, friends, or money. She even sent some to the seaside to recuperate, at her own expense.

Florence was a wonderful nurse. But in her efficiency, there was a streak of coldness that frightened some people a little. It was as if the overly emotional experiences she had had with her mother and Parthenope had made her wary of softness. And softness was not going to make efficient hospitals.

She felt she needed to use her razor-sharp mind to its fullest to reform them.

In a very short time, Nightingale was known as the leading expert in her field, and work at the hospital on Harley Street was simply not enough to occupy her.

She prepared well-researched and well-presented papers on the many problems of England's hospitals. More and more people involved with hospitals and nursing came to respect her and agree with her.

Nightingale, wisely, stayed away from her family. She was no longer a puppet who jumped with every jerk of the string. She had a job to do, and she was going to do it. Toward the end of 1854, she drew up plans for recruiting farmers' daughters to be trained as nurses as women were at Kaiserswerth.

At a time when most women had scarcely begun to gain equal rights, Florence Nightingale was working as an equal with men.

The Crimean War

Meanwhile, all England was reading of the triumphs of the British Army in the Crimea. Britain and France were fighting to support their Turkish allies in a war against Russia. Nightingale did not suspect, as she read of the army's victories, that she would soon be joining them. She, too, would fight — not against the Russians, but against disease and the disorganization, filth, cold, and hunger that went with it.

Florence Nightingale's experience, intelligence, courage, and determination were about to be put to their greatest test in the next few years. They would change not only the way people thought of nurses and nursing but the way people thought of women.

As in all wars, many human beings were to die horrible and unnecessary deaths before the Crimean War was over. Yet something good came out of the horror — a greater respect for the common soldier and wide-ranging reforms both in military organization and in the way hospitals were run. Florence Nightingale was the key figure in these reforms.

The British Army was the best in the world. It could never be beaten. Or so everyone in Britain believed in 1854. The soldiers, in their bright, clean

In 1854, an outbreak of cholera swept through the London slums. Florence volunteered to help, and she tended filthy, terrified prostitutes and drunks with as much care as she gave her patients at the Institution for the Care of Sick Gentlewomen. When there was nothing she could do to help, she held many of them in her arms while they died. Decades later, she would campaign for better sanitary conditions in the slums and London would never again be swept by cholera.

uniforms, marched to ships that were to take them to the Crimean Peninsula, jutting into the Black Sea. Banners waved in the sun, bands played, drummer boys proudly led the parade.

But this gallant army was to be defeated — by disease, lack of organization, cold, and hunger.

The British troops crossed the Black Sea to a campsite at Varna, Bulgaria, to help the Turks, who were under siege. Varna was a notorious breeding ground for cholera, and an epidemic of the disease broke out almost immediately. Night after night, the British soldiers could hear the splashing sound of corpses being tossed into the bay. Within three weeks, sickness rendered the army just about useless.

The British forces then turned their attention to the main objective of Sebastopol. The men needed to cross the Black Sea from Varna to Sebastopol, on the Crimean shore. But there were not enough ships to take both the army and its equipment. The military leaders decided to transport only the troops. There had not been any advance planning for moving all the people and equipment needed to fight well. Left behind were pack animals, tents, cooking stoves,

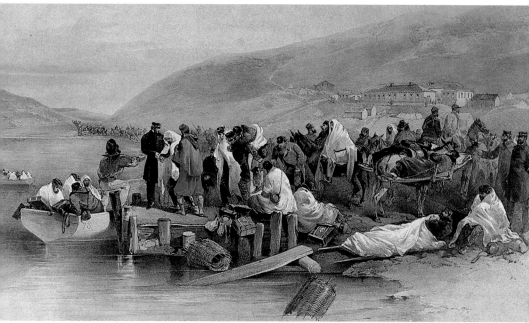

medical supplies, bedding, and many other supplies.

Only twenty-one wagons had been brought for the transportation of thirty thousand soldiers. On board the ships, there was hardly any food or water, and cholera continued to spread.

When the men landed in September, many soldiers were ordered to leave their packs behind. Besides, they were too weak to carry them. The lack of supplies had already driven them to drink from the filthy puddles on the beaches. Britain's proud soldiers writhed on the ground. They were tortured by diarrhea and dysentery.

The agony of victory

Thus Britain's first battles in the Crimea were fought by men exhausted by disease and racked with hunger and thirst. Nevertheless, this army of invalids had managed to cross the Alma, storm the heights above the river, and force the Russian army to retreat into the city of Sebastopol. Naturally, some men were wounded in the fighting.

It might have been better for them if they had been killed outright. All the medical supplies had been left at the campsite at Varna. There were no bandages, no splints, no anesthetics of any kind! There were no candles or lamps, so the surgeons sometimes operated guided only by moonlight. Many patients lay on straw-covered manure on open ground.

Eventually, the sick and wounded were packed into hospital ships to make the crossing back to a base at Scutari, in Turkey. But by the time the wounded began to arrive, the hospital was already filled to overflowing with cholera patients. These soldiers had been brought down by disease before any of them even came close to gunfire.

Since the main hospital at Scutari was already filled with over one thousand cholera patients, British officers had to use an old, run-down, and filthy barracks as a makeshift hospital.

The Barrack Hospital could provide no food, because it had no kitchen. There was no linen, which hardly mattered because there were no beds. There were no cups that caretakers could use to bring a sip of

Opposite, top: The women say goodbye to soldiers dressed in their finery. The troops were too confident as they set sail for the Crimean War. Within a week of their arrival and before the first battle had been fought, over one thousand men had died of disease.

Opposite, bottom: The first battles were disasters for the British. Two thousand men were killed in the Battle of Inkerman alone. The wounded endured great hardship. They were taken on crude litters to the coast, where they waited days for a ship to transport them to the hospital on the south coast of the Black Sea. Even if they survived the journey, many had wounds so badly infected that they would eventually die.

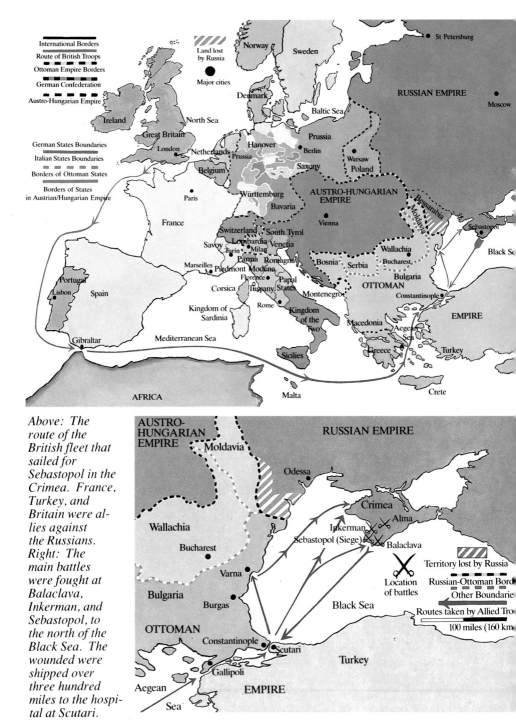

Map legend (top map)

- International Borders
- Route of British Troops
- Ottoman Empire Borders
- German Confederation
- Austro-Hungarian Empire

Land lost by Russia

Major cities

- German States Boundaries
- Italian States Boundaries
- Borders of Ottoman States
- Borders of States in Austrian/Hungarian Empire

Top map labels:

St Petersburg
Norway
Sweden
RUSSIAN EMPIRE
Moscow
Denmark
Baltic Sea
Ireland
North Sea
Great Britain
Prussia
Hanover
Berlin
London
Netherlands
Prussia
Warsaw
Belgium
Saxony
Poland
Paris
Württemberg
AUSTRO-HUNGARIAN EMPIRE
Bessarabia
France
Bavaria
Vienna
Moldavia
Sebastopol
Switzerland
South Tyrol
Lombardia
Venetia
Savoy
Turin
Milan
Wallachia
Black Sea
Parma
Romagna
Bucharest
Marseilles
Piedmont
Modena
Bosnia
Serbia
Bulgaria
Portugal
Florence
Papal
Tuscany
States
OTTOMAN
Lisbon
Spain
Corsica
Rome
Constantinople
EMPIRE
Kingdom of Sardinia
Kingdom of the Two
Montenegro
Macedonia
Aegean Sea
Turkey
Gibraltar
Mediterranean Sea
Sicilies
Greece
AFRICA
Malta
Crete

Caption (left column)

Above: The route of the British fleet that sailed for Sebastopol in the Crimea. France, Turkey, and Britain were allies against the Russians. Right: The main battles were fought at Balaclava, Inkerman, and Sebastopol, to the north of the Black Sea. The wounded were shipped over three hundred miles to the hospital at Scutari.

Bottom map labels:

AUSTRO-HUNGARIAN EMPIRE
RUSSIAN EMPIRE
Moldavia
Odessa
Crimea
Alma
Wallachia
Inkerman
Sebastopol (Siege)
Balaclava
Bucharest
Varna
Bulgaria
Burgas
Black Sea
OTTOMAN
Constantinople
Scutari
Gallipoli
Turkey
Aegean
EMPIRE
Sea

Bottom map legend:

Territory lost by Russia
Location of battles
Russian-Ottoman Border
Other Boundaries
Routes taken by Allied Troops
100 miles (160 km)

water to men who were parched with fever. There were no tables or chairs. There were a few doctors available, but they had no operating tables. The Barrack Hospital was nothing but a skeleton of a building, full of men in agony lying on the bare floor. Most of them were half-wrapped in blankets caked with blood and filth. Filling the air were the sounds of crying out — from the men who still had the strength — for something to drink.

News from the front

To hardened soldiers, this was nothing new. But to the rest of Great Britain, the news came as a great shock.

Something had to be done. And fast. Britain's allies, the French, had more surgeons. They also had the Sisters of Charity to help in the field. The British had no one. Who could be sent to put things right?

To Sidney Herbert, Nightingale's old, faithful friend and now Britain's Secretary at War, there was only one answer — Nightingale herself. On October 15, he wrote to Nightingale asking her to organize a body of nurses and to go out to Scutari as soon as possible.

Here was the work that Nightingale felt God had intended her to do. She knew, as Herbert knew, that it was a job only she could do.

To Nightingale's surprise, even her mother and sister supported her. "It is a great and noble work," wrote her sister Parthe. "One cannot but believe she was intended for it."

Nightingale accepted Herbert's proposal and, at the age of thirty-four, she was appointed Superintendent of the Female Nursing Establishment of the English General Hospitals in Turkey. But she was going to need help. So it was decided that forty nurses would go with her.

But finding suitable nurses was not going to be easy. With a great deal of thought and effort, however, Nightingale got together a group of thirty-eight women — an ill-assorted group but the best she could get. Some were professional nurses, some were nuns — the most efficient being five sisters from a Roman Catholic convent. On October 21, 1854, the party sailed from London.

"Then there was the question of Army hospitals though this was hardly a question. There were none. If a battlefield happened to be near a city, as was the field of Waterloo, civic hospitals were available but were far too small to cope with the enormous influx of the wounded and dying. Further, there were no Army nurses. There were orderlies, but many of them were pensioners so old and infirm they could scarcely lift a stretcher."
Elizabeth Burton,
from The Early
Victorians at Home

CARRYING THE FROST-BITTEN TO BALACLAVA.

Nightingale arrives in Scutari

Demoralized, frostbitten troops are carried back to Balaclava. Many died on the way to the hospital — often frozen upright in the saddle. Even when they got back to base, their chances of surviving were slim. Infection and inadequate food would kill thousands of them.

On November 5, 1854, Nightingale and her fellow nurses entered the Barrack Hospital at Scutari.

Nightingale had been told about what she would find. But none of the descriptions had prepared her for what she saw — chaos and misery everywhere.

The bare corridors led to filthy wards. The central courtyard was a morass of stinking mud. There was rubbish and dirt everywhere. There were *four miles of beds* — if one could call them that. The wounded lay only a foot or so apart. It was a hotbed of infectious disease crawling with vermin. Most patients who died in this "hospital" died not just from the wounds or diseases that sent them there but from diseases they got from being amid all the filth.

But Nightingale, for all her ability to improve this, had to tread carefully. All medical staff were firmly under the control of the military authorities. One wrong move and she might find herself, and her nurses, ordered home.

Organization had broken down. Everything required an application form, a permission slip, signed by two doctors. Precious foodstuffs were lost or rotting because the correct applications had not been made or because no one would take the responsibility of issuing them. Any officials not applying in the correct way were in serious trouble, but many were never told just what way *was* correct.

Many officers regarded the solders under them as "scum," "brutes," and "blackguards." They warned Florence not to "spoil" them. She found herself confronted by officers who cared more about paperwork than people — and by Lord Stratford Canning, the British Ambassador to Constantinople (now Istanbul) in Turkey. He had tremendous influence, but he lived in luxury in a palace and simply ignored the filth, pain, and misery that the soldiers endured "within sight of his windows," as Florence noted.

Rules and regulations

The Barrack Hospital lacked the equipment that was essential for decent medical care. No operating tables. No medical supplies. No furniture. Rats and fleas infested the nurses' room — and there were no lamps or candles. At night, the women lay in darkness, listening to the scampering of rats' feet.

All but one of the doctors resented Nightingale and ignored her. They considered even decent bedding and hot soup "preposterous luxuries." She knew she must win their trust before she could be effective. She gave her nurses careful instructions. Despite the anguish of having to leave the wounded, they had to wait until they were officially asked to help.

On November 6, a huge new group of men arrived who had been terribly wounded at the Battle of Balaclava. Still Nightingale restrained her nurses. They found what linen they could and made bandages, slings, stump rests, pillows, and shirts for the men. Then they waited.

When she was asked to follow military rules, Nightingale forced herself to accept the regulations. Only in the kitchen could she herself take control. What she found there disgusted her. There were no saucepans or kettles. Tea was made in pots in which meat had just been boiled.

The Scutari Barrack Hospital before the twenty thousand wounded men arrived. Scutari was literally a barracks, not a hospital. There were four miles of long, dirty halls that would become four miles of crowded beds. There were rats, leaking roofs, and no running water. The lavatories were blocked and overflowed into the wards. Nightingale arrived with almost forty nurses — only twenty would survive.

Roll Call, *the famous painting by Lady Butler, wife of an officer. She portrayed the suffering and courage of ordinary men caught up in war. This picture depicts an officer counting the survivors after the Battle of Balaclava.*

Opposite: The blinded, crippled, and wounded struggle back from the front, helping their friends as best they can. Their lives will now depend on good food and good, clean conditions in the hospital — which Nightingale was fighting to provide.

Nightingale got to work. She had brought wine, soup extract, and portable stoves with her. She stuck strictly to every rule so that no one could object to her actions. Nothing was given to a patient without a signed slip from a doctor, but gradually the poor, sick, hungry men were eating food that did them good instead of making them even more ill.

No one knows how long this situation would have gone on — but on November 9, the doctors gave in. A great tide of sick and wounded swept into Scutari. The doctors and officials were forced to acknowledge Nightingale's existence and to accept help from her and her nurses.

The great task begins

The new flood of wounded, dying humanity began when the British suffered a defeat at the Battle of Balaclava on October 25. The nearby camp was soon a quagmire of filth. Bodies and the amputated limbs of the wounded floated in the quiet sea. Stench — and

When they read of the suffering, the people of Britain donated shiploads of sheets, bandages, and food. The problem was that the incompetent medical officers would not release them. Many of the soldiers called Nightingale "The Lady with the Hammer" after she broke into the supply rooms to get materials for the patients.

cholera — swept through the war-devastated camp.

The Battle of Inkerman followed. Although it was a British victory, it added to the wounded. Winter was setting in. Men clawed at the frozen ground with bleeding hands to find a few dead roots to burn. There was nowhere to cook a hot meal. There was nowhere to sleep but on frozen mud. The only dirt road leading out of the area was impassable.

Disease, gangrene, death — it seemed like hell on Earth. Now the flood of victims was being sent to swell the huge numbers already at Scutari.

Nightingale had to admire the military medical staff. They were on their feet for twenty-four hours at a time. But their heroic efforts were hardly enough to do much good amid the constant influx of patients. Men were jammed into every space, lying on bare boards with their heads on their boots for lack of beds or pillows. Nightingale estimated that more than one thousand men were suffering from diarrhea, and there were only twenty chamber pots. The chamber pots were supposed to be emptied into vast vats, but the orderlies dodged this awful job, and the pots were sometimes left for twenty-four hours at a time. The stench could be smelled outside the hospital walls.

As if this misery were not enough, on November 14 a tremendous storm broke and carried away whatever tents the army had erected, leaving many men without shelter of any kind. Every single ship in the harbor was sunk, including one that had arrived the day before, loaded with desperately needed warm clothes and other supplies.

Nightingale takes over

By the end of November, the hospital administration had broken down. Officials were grateful for Nightingale's presence, for she had money from British charities. She also could get essential supplies.

She took over quietly, determined to avoid confrontation if she could.

The patients' clothes had not been washed for five weeks, so every shirt was crawling with vermin. Nightingale ordered boilers, and boilers were installed. The chamber pots and vats were emptied and cleaned.

An idealized picture painted to show the concern Nightingale had for each man in her care, striving to make each one as comfortable as possible under the circumstances.

Many of the troops disembarked at Varna in Bulgaria. The site was notorious for cholera, and the disease swept through the army. Ultimately, over one thousand men with cholera were sent back to Scutari.

The Thin Red Line, *the 93rd Highlanders at Balaclava, painted by Caton Woodville. During the war, the allied forces of Britain, France, and Turkey lost between them eighty-two thousand soldiers in battle, but disease and the terrible Crimean winter killed even more men than sword or gunfire did.*

Nightingale gave great attention to detail. She made an inventory of every single item that was needed and got them — trays, tables, clocks, towels, soap, cups, plates, and eating utensils.

At the beginning of December, one of the British commanders, Lord Raglan, had warned Nightingale that he was sending five hundred more wounded and sick to the already overcrowded hospital. Nightingale needed space badly. One wing of the hospital had been damaged by fire and left to fall into near ruin. Nightingale pressed to have the wing put into good order. After endless difficulties with Lord Stratford and the Turkish workers hired to do the repairs, she took it upon herself to get the work done, paying for it out of her own money and donated funds.

Necessary goods that should have come through the army's supply system now came through Miss Nightingale. The army officials were angry, but Nightingale ignored them and went doggedly on.

"Calamity unparalleled"

The winter brought horror upon horror. In January 1855, the plight of the wounded became even worse. It was, Nightingale wrote, "calamity unparalleled in the history of calamity." The number of patients multiplied to a terrifying degree, and already there were twelve thousand men in the hospital. Nightingale was fighting great odds, but she focused her energies on what had to be done. She wrote carefully reasoned plans for the reorganization of the hospitals, dealing with both the present and the future.

One of the greatest anxieties was the ever-rising number of deaths at the Barrack Hospital, despite the improvements that had been made. Soldiers were more likely to die at the Barrack Hospital than they were in the crude, freezing regimental hospitals on the heights outside Sebastopol. At the end of December, an epidemic broke out. Four surgeons, three nurses, a supply official, and hundreds of soldiers had already died from an epidemic that started before the new year.

Now things were getting even worse. Whatever was done, the grim numbers kept rising.

British newspapers carried news of this appalling

state of affairs. People began to demand that the whole tragedy of the Crimea be investigated. The wave of public indignation forced the government to appoint and send a Sanitary Commission to investigate the hospitals and camps at the end of February 1855.

Reform at the Barrack Hospital

The Commission inspected the Barrack Hospital from top to bottom. It was little wonder the death rate was so high. The entire building was standing on a network of badly decaying sewers. As a result, it was soaked through with decay, filth, and disease. The water supply was infected, and even the movement of the air had carried death through the crowded wards.

In the first two weeks of coping with this horror, workers removed 556 handcarts and large baskets of garbage and buried twenty-six assorted dead animals, including two dead horses.

Conditions at the hospital improved. But bungling and lack of organization meant that terrible, costly mistakes still occurred. In one instance, a transport ship was being loaded with several hundred wounded soldiers. For two weeks, they lay on the bare decks with no protection from the winter weather except their tattered coats and filthy blankets. The officer responsible was later reprimanded, only to be appointed Senior Medical Officer at the Barrack Hospital! It shocked Nightingale when officials who had opposed every reform and blocked her work at every turn were often rewarded, particularly after the war.

"The Lady With the Lamp"

By the spring of 1855, Nightingale was exhausted. At times she was on her knees for eight hours straight, dressing wounds. She had none of the drugs or dressings of a modern hospital ward. She had to make do with what little she had.

What kept her going was the incredible bravery of the men. They tried never to complain, never to betray their agony, fear, and homesickness. If Nightingale had in the past gained a reputation for coldness, no one except stubborn officials saw it now. The men always remembered her patience, her kindness — even her

Once the situation at Scutari was under control, Nightingale visited the medical stations nearer the battle areas. She rode out in all kinds of weather — and paid the price by becoming dangerously ill.

"What a comfort it was to see her pass even. She would speak to one, and nod and smile to as many more: but she could not do it all you know. We lay there by [the] hundreds; but we could kiss her shadow as it fell and lay our heads on the pillow again content."

A soldier in the Barrack Hospital

good cheer. She stood by them when they were forced to endure surgery. She gave them new hope just by moving among them on her rounds, speaking to one, smiling at another.

If she couldn't see them during the day, she made her rounds at night, lighting her way along the four miles of beds with a Turkish lamp. One soldier wrote that the men were so devoted to her that some even kissed her shadow on the wall as she passed. In turn, Nightingale's respect for them would in years to come forever change European attitudes toward "common" soldiers. Long after Scutari, Florence Nightingale would still be fighting to improve their lot.

Crimean fever

Nightingale kept working on at everything that came her way. Once the Barrack Hospital was in satisfactory condition, she decided it was time to go to the Crimean hospitals. There, at last, she paid the price of long hours and worry. Her strength failed her while she was inspecting conditions at Balaclava, and she was diagnosed as having "Crimean fever." For two weeks, she lay at the edge of death, but even when she was delirious, she wrote and wrote and wrote — lists, orders, recommendations.

When she was finally able to leave her room, people were shocked at the change in her. She was pale and thin; her nose was prominent in her drawn face. She would never again be as strong and vigorous as she had been.

Trouble met her as she went back to work. The army, the nurses, and the nuns all seemed to be having their own private wars. Their petty disputes were causing big problems — which they left Nightingale to solve.

Her family decided that someone must go to be with Florence. Aunt Mai volunteered, and on September 16, 1855, she arrived in Scutari. She was horrified by Florence's frailty and pallor and by the bitter feuds and pettiness that surrounded her. She got busy helping Florence with the paper work. Of her niece, she wrote: "The public generally imagine[s] her by the soldier's bedside. . . . How easy, how satisfactory if that were all."

But more and more people in Britain knew that that was not all — and more and more wanted to do something to help Florence in her ambitious task.

The Nightingale Fund

In England, Nightingale was called "the light of the Crimea." The country was bursting with Nightingale souvenirs — mugs and plates, pottery busts, poems and, unfortunately, wildly inaccurate biographies.

A racehorse was named after her. So were many ships, including a lifeboat. But Nightingale, level-headed as ever, was totally unmoved. She had lived all those months amid stark reality, and she knew how much still needed to be done.

People donated money to buy an expensive testimonial gift for Florence — "something of the teapot and bracelet variety," as Parthe wrote wryly. But so much money was being donated that it was decided to set up a Nightingale Fund to help establish an institute

"What the horrors of war are no one can imagine. They are not wounds and blood, and fever, spotted and low, and dysentery, and heat and famine. They are intoxication, drunken brutality, demoralization and disorder on the part of the inferior: jealousies, meanness, indifference, selfish brutality on the part of the superior."

Florence Nightingale

The remains of an army go home. They had marched to the troopships with bands playing and flags flying. They had won their battles — but had been defeated by dirt, disease, and bad organization. Nightingale had saved many but her pioneering work was to ensure that thousands more in the years to come were given the care they deserved.

for training nurses. British soldiers were urged to contribute a day's pay to the fund. They gave almost nine thousand British pounds. (This, accounting for today's prices, equals about $380,000 in US money.)

Florence's mother, Fanny, was overcome with emotion. She wrote to tell Florence how proud she was of her. And Florence, setting aside the past, wrote back, "My reputation has not been a boon in my work; but if you have been pleased that is enough."

War of words

But not everyone supported Florence. In December, the Chief of Medical Staff of the British Expeditionary Army, Sir John Hall, sent the British War Office a report that accused Nightingale of insubordination and her nurses of dishonesty, extravagance, disobedience, inefficiency, and immorality.

It was a pack of lies, and Nightingale was furious.

A great battle of words, letters, and meetings broke out between the government and the people trying to blacken Nightingale's name.

But at the beginning of 1856, a special commission appointed to investigate the supply scandals in the Crimea submitted its report to Parliament. It confirmed everything that Nightingale had reported.

Incredibly, however, even after the report shocked the nation, Hall was made a Knight Commander of the Bath, K.C.B. "Knight of the Crimean Burial grounds, I suppose," wrote Nightingale bitterly. "I am in a state of chronic rage. I, who saw the men come down through all that long[,] long dreadful winter without other covering than a dirty blanket and a pair of old regimental trousers, when we knew the stores were bursting with warm clothing, living skeletons devoured by vermin, ulcerated, hopeless, speechless, dying like the Greeks as they wrapped their heads in their blankets and spoke never a word. . . . Can we hear of the promotion of the men who caused this colossal calamity, we who saw it?"

Ultimately, however, Florence was vindicated. On March 16, 1856, an order was issued to Britain's military authorities. It read: "Miss Nightingale is recognized by Her Majesty's Government as General Superintendent of the Female Nursing Establishment of the military hospitals of the Army."

All the military officers who had ignored her now had no choice but to respect her. Her enemies were defeated at one blow.

Return to England

Nightingale was exhausted but triumphant. Soon after, on March 30, 1856, peace was declared. The fighting was at an end, but the threat of disease was not. It was essential to get the men home before the summer came — with the heat that bred cholera. On July 16, 1856, the last patient left the Barrack Hospital. Nightingale's work in the Crimea was over.

On July 28, she and Aunt Mai sailed for France. Nightingale left Aunt Mai in Paris and secretly went on to England alone. She wanted to avoid the crowds and the grand receptions all Britain was planning for her return. On the morning after her arrival, she went to the Convent of the Bermondsey Nuns and spent the morning there in prayer and quiet. In the afternoon she

"Two figures emerged from the Crimea as heroic, the soldier and the nurse. In each case a transformation in public estimation took place, and in each case the transformation was due to Miss Nightingale."
Cecil Woodham-Smith, from Florence Nightingale

"No one can feel for the army as I do. People must have seen that long dreadful winter to know what it was. I can never forget."
Florence Nightingale

Sentimental souvenirs of Florence. Many models show Florence with wounded soldiers.

went quietly home to Lea Hurst, one of her family's country homes.

Even if the war was over, even if awards and praises were heaped on her, Nightingale could not forget. She feared she had failed. The capable, efficient organizer, apparently unbreakable in her resolve, wrote in her private diary:

"Oh my poor men; I am a bad mother to come home and leave you in your Crimean graves — 73 per cent in 8 regiments in 6 months from disease alone — who thinks of that now?"

Over and over, on as many papers as she could find, she also wrote: "I can never forget."

Nightingale the heroine

Nightingale was exhausted by her struggles in the Crimea. She was only thirty-six but she felt her work was over. Now she could rest, recover, and have a little time to herself. She did not realize that the main work of her life was just beginning. She had nearly forty years of accomplishments ahead of her.

During the first months after the war, she was drowning in congratulatory letters, hysterical admiration, requests for money and jobs, and even proposals of marriage — not much different from what many modern film and television stars must put up with! But she hated being a celebrity. So she signed no autographs, granted no interviews, attended no public functions. Only the humblest and most sincere letter writers were honored with her personal replies. Her sister wrote most other letters to admirers. People stopped expecting her to react; her life quieted down.

The Victorians created a sentimental image of Florence Nightingale. To them, she was the "Lady With the Lamp" — a kind, gentle, softhearted woman who bent over the beds of sick and dying men to offer comfort and hope. But that was only one side of Nightingale's character. She was also strong-willed and independent, intelligent, and diplomatic. When the "Lady With the Lamp" took up a cause, she was a force to be reckoned with.

The Crimean War revealed plenty of causes for Florence to take up. She already knew that nurses needed to be trained. But she had to find a way to make nursing a respectable profession, with standards of conduct and achievement that all nurses would have to measure up to. Hospitals had to be changed, too — many of the deaths at Scutari were caused by the atrocious hospital conditions and nothing else. Nightingale had spent years studying hospitals all over Europe. No one knew more about what went on in hospitals and exactly what had to be changed.

In the years to come, she would tackle these problems and many others, from the administration of the poorhouses in Liverpool, England, to the health and living conditions in the entire country of India.

For now, she wanted to change the British Army.

The memories of Scutari and Balaclava haunted her, but all that suffering had taught the army medical authorities nothing. The system that had been at the root of the chaos and misery of the Crimea continued in every British army barracks and hospital. Nightingale could not ignore it.

Below: Victorian romantic sentiments clouded the real achievements of Florence Nightingale. Note the picture on the left, with Florence walking moonlit wards clutching an armful of roses! The incompetent officers who had faced the tough, determined, uncompromising nurse in the Crimea did not remember this side of Florence Nightingale.

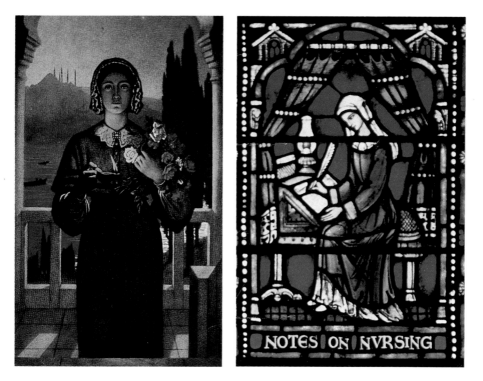

NOTES ON NVRSING

Queen Victoria helps

Then a wonderful opportunity came. Queen Victoria wanted to hear Nightingale's story from her own lips. She began preparing evidence to convince the queen of the need for army reform. She worked furiously. When she was not writing to military experts, she visited military hospitals and barracks. Arriving home, she would start writing again. Often, in the next thirty years, she would work twenty-two hours at a time.

In September, just two months after her return from the Crimea, she went to Balmoral Castle, in Scotland, for a meeting with the queen and her husband, Prince Albert. They were delighted with her and listened carefully to everything she told them.

They asked her back again and again.

It was a real beginning, but Nightingale now had to win over Britain's chief government ministers. As an outsider, she could not change basic practices in Britain's army without being an important politician. And as a woman of her time, she could not be an official. The only way open to her was to work through some of the leading officials of the time. So she did this. Sidney Herbert and at least four other British government leaders devoted much of their spare time to her causes. They respected her as *the* expert in hospital conditions. They enjoyed working for her because of her gentle but methodical approach.

The negotiations brought six months more of tiring hospital visits, persuasion, and writing — driving Nightingale to exhaustion.

Army reform

Finally, in May 1857, a royal commission to study the whole question of the army medical service began its work. The cost to Nightingale was enormous. She had been doing this grueling work because she felt it was vital, not because she liked it. She was more brilliant in argument than ever, more efficient, more knowledgeable, more persistent and penetrating in her reasoning, scrupulously just, mathematically accurate. But she was pushing herself at the expense of all joy.

The summer of 1857 was a nightmare. Not only was she working day and night to educate members of the commission she had fought so hard to bring into existence, but she was writing her own confidential report about her Crimean War experiences. All this time Parthe and Mrs. Nightingale continued to live the conventional lives of upper-class Victorian women while Florence drove herself beyond what even she thought was the limit.

It took Nightingale only six months to complete her confidential report, *Notes on Matters affecting the Health, Efficiency and Hospital Administration of the British Army*. It was a clear, thorough volume of one thousand pages. Everything she had learned from the Crimea was there, and every statement, every recommendation she made, was backed by hard evidence.

Nightingale was basically arguing for prevention rather than cure. This was a new idea then. Many authorities felt it was revolutionary and perhaps positively crazy. They opposed Nightingale's plan.

She needed to prove that the soldiers were dying

Below: The commission was made up entirely of men, not surprisingly for that time period. It was established in 1857 to study the army medical service. Several of the members not only admired Nightingale but took instruction directly from her. Her criticisms of the army were merciless.

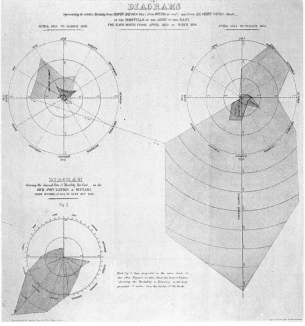

Above left: A cartoon of the day, showing how army recruits were seen by the press — as drunken, lazy oafs. Florence saw them differently, as ordinary people, driven by poverty into the army and then treated badly.

Above right: Florence's detailed way of presenting her research. She showed that for every soldier killed in battle in the Crimean War, seven died of infections and diseases that they need not have fallen victim to. Better food, cleanliness, and good ventilation could prevent disease and death.

because of their living conditions. She had inspected dozens of hospitals and barracks and exposed them as damp, filthy, and unventilated, with tainted water. She showed that the soldiers' diet was poor. She collected statistics proving that the death rate for young British soldiers *in peacetime* was double that of Britain's civilian population.

Even though the army took only the fittest young men, at least 1,500 of them died each year from neglect, poor food, and disease.

"Our soldiers," she said, "enlist to death in the barracks." This became her battle cry.

The public was also on her side. The more her foes dragged their feet, the greater the pressure for reform.

She did not win an outright victory against her opponents, but changes were made. Barracks were rebuilt. Within only three years, the death rate among British soldiers stationed within their own country was cut in half.

The work with the commission was over, but Nightingale continued studying, planning, and pressing for army medical reform for the next thirty years.

Collapse

On August 11, Nightingale collapsed. She had not been alone for four years. She longed for peace and quiet. She had not eaten solid food for four weeks. Living only on tea, she was so ill that someone wrote her obituary in advance.

But Nightingale didn't have time to die. Instead, she left London, although she could not leave her work. When she returned to London, Aunt Mai came with her and stood by Florence as she had in the Crimea. With her help, Nightingale was able to turn the tables on her sister and mother. When they threatened to visit, she had an "attack," and Aunt Mai wrote, saying that Florence's life "hung by a thread" so they must stay away. And stay away they finally did.

A proposal for Parthe

Nightingale's attempt to keep her family at a distance was aided by Sir Harry Verney. In the summer of 1857, after a series of social calls, he proposed marriage. Nightingale turned him down.

But Parthe did not. Sir Harry transferred his affections to Florence's older sister, and by 1858, they were engaged. Parthe and her mother busied themselves with wedding preparations.

After the wedding, in June 1858, Nightingale moved into the quiet annex of London's Burlington Hotel. She no longer saw friends or went to parties or concerts. Aunt Mai and her son-in-law, Arthur Hugh Clough, looked after her. Nightingale made plans for her funeral, but from a semireclining position on her sofa, she managed to work harder than she'd ever worked before.

People now asked that she investigate civilian hospitals, which she thought just had to be in better condition than any military hospital. But she found them to be worse than military hospitals. In 1859, she published *Notes on Hospitals*. It told the world why people feared entering hospitals — and how things could be made better.

She set forth a then-revolutionary theory. By simply improving hospital construction and maintenance, she said, hospital deaths could be greatly reduced.

A benign Florence Nightingale with some of her nurses. One of the secrets of her success was that she was a perfectionist. She had seen the results of sloppy planning in the Crimea and for the rest of her life she fought for high standards. No detail was too small. She had an opinion on everything, from the width of operating room doors to the shade of the paint. Somehow she passed her passion for caring and perfectionism on to others.

More windows, better ventilation, improved drainage, less cramped conditions, and regular scrubbing of floors, walls, and bed frames were basic measures every hospital could take at once.

Nightingale soon became an expert on the building of hospitals. Medical experts and foreign rulers sent her hospital plans, asking her approval and advice. Hospitals all over the world were soon being built according to her plans. From her sofa in London, she wrote hundreds and hundreds of letters inquiring about sinks and saucepans, locks and laundry rooms. No detail was too small for her careful thought. She had careful plans for the most efficient way to distribute clean linen, the best method to keep food hot, the correct number of inches between beds. She intended to change the way hospitals were run in every way. After all, people's lives depended on these things.

Florence Nightingale succeeded. She would continue to advise people on hospital plans for over forty years. Today's hospitals, with their flowers, recreation rooms, and their bright, fresh, and cheerful wards, are a direct result of her work.

Notes on Nursing

One of the hospitals she advised was St. Thomas's, in London. As she talked with its board members about their plans to build a new hospital, she decided it would be a good place to establish a school for nurses.

While the negotiations proceeded, she wrote a small book about nursing to be used by ordinary women. Published in 1859, just three years after she came back from the Crimea, *Notes on Nursing: What it is and what it is not* was an instant success. Even today, it is her best known work out of all the books, pamphlets, and articles she wrote.

Like all Nightingale's work, *Notes on Nursing* was revolutionary, but it contained nothing that is not accepted today as basic good hygiene.

Nightingale not only described with great sensitivity the suffering, both physical and mental, of a sick person, but also attacked the conventional notion of a nurse. "It seems a commonly received idea among men, and even among women themselves," she wrote, "that it requires nothing but a disappointment in love, or incapacity in other things, to turn a woman into a good nurse."

The Nightingale nurses

To get rid of this silly idea, Nightingale needed to present the world with a different kind of nurse. Many doctors of the time were against all professional training of nurses. They felt that would-be nurses could learn by experience and simple instruction on the spot. Many men, including supposedly intelligent male doctors, still regarded women as the weaker and less intelligent sex — even with the example of Nightingale before their eyes. But six months after publishing *Notes on Nursing,* Florence was able, with the forty-five thousand British pounds from the Nightingale Fund (about $2 million in modern US currency), to open her training school for nurses, attached to St. Thomas's Hospital.

"Nightingale nurses" were to be trained to train others and to take jobs where they could bring Florence's high standards to other places.

"A nurse returning to the north found a luncheon-basket waiting in her railway carriage; another, who had been ill, received a diet sheet with the note: 'get the things out of my money.' Run-down nurses were invited to convalesce for a weekend in bed. Each probationer was invited, by herself, to tea, and given a present, often a cake. One of the young women, dressed in her best to obey the summons, heard at the last moment that the poverty of the guest's attire determined the size of the cake. Hastily changing into her oldest clothes, she returned from the tea-party with a cake large enough to feed all thirty-six probationers."

Elspeth Huxley,
from Florence Nightingale

All candidates were hand-picked and had to have character references. They were issued plain but neat uniforms. Discipline was strict, but each student nurse had her own room. Nightingale sent flowers, books, maps, and pictures to make the school a pleasant place in which to live and work. No nurse had ever before been given a chance to study in this way.

Within a few months, requests for Nightingale nurses were flooding in.

The Nightingale Training School was succeeding.

Soon it would become world-famous. Within fifteen years, hospitals all over the world were asking for Nightingale nurses to start new schools.

By 1867, a group of six sailed to Sydney, Australia. By 1887, the fiftieth anniversary of Florence Nightingale's first call to her life's work, nurses at most of the major hospitals in the British Isles, Canada, Germany, Sweden, and the United States had been trained at the Nightingale school.

Once, nursing implied casual sexual habits and drunkenness, but today it has become one of the most respected professions in the world. That change is largely because of Florence Nightingale and her single-minded determination and her endless work.

Today, nurses are highly qualified and respected. Their public image is a world away from what it was in the mid-nineteenth century, when Nightingale started out. She is recognized around the world as the pioneer of modern nursing. Fewer people know about her success at reforming medical practices.

A time of loss

In 1860, Nightingale was to find herself more and more alone. First, one of her close friends, Dr. Thomas Alexander, died suddenly. He had been working on new British Army medical regulations in response to Florence's call for reform. Then Aunt Mai returned to her own family.

Finally, Sidney Herbert became very ill. By June 1861, he was so ill he told Florence that he planned to resign from the British War Office. Blinded by her yearning for further progress, she could not forgive him. She felt he had betrayed her.

Two months later, Sidney Herbert died. His last words were, "Poor Florence . . . poor Florence . . . our joint work unfinished."

Nightingale was horrified to hear the news. He had endured so much of her anger and reproach, while working unceasingly for her causes. "And his angelic temper with me," she said, "I shall never forget."

Herbert's death was a great loss to Nightingale, because he was both a great and dear friend and was her strongest supporter at the War Office. She had always worked with and through him. Without him, she was shut out. His death meant her cause of army reform came to a halt. As Florence recovered from her grief, she knew she would have to direct her vast knowledge and her passion for change elsewhere.

In 1861, the US Civil War had broken out. President Abraham Lincoln's Secretary of War, Simon Cameron, asked Florence for help in organizing hospitals for the sick and wounded of the North. When it seemed that Britain might become involved, British officials also asked for her help.

In order to get her materials organized for two countries on time, Nightingale worked day and night. As might have been expected, she collapsed again. By Christmas Eve 1861, she was not expected to live, but by January 1862, she could sit up in bed. However, she could not walk. For six years, she had to be carried from room to room.

Yet she had a constant stream of important visitors. Politicians and hospital administrators and others all called on her for advice or help. She did all her work from her bed or sofa, usually surrounded by at least

three pet cats! She never lost her eye for detail and seemed never to rest. She wrote letters, books, and reports well into the early hours of the morning. Some of her letters and other papers still have the paw prints of her cats.

For much of the rest of her life — almost fifty years — Nightingale would often be in poor health. When she was exhausted or when she became upset, usually because of her family, her condition would worsen. We do not always know exactly what was wrong with her health, but she suffered from weakness, fatigue, and breathlessness.

As she got older, she refused to see most visitors unless they were connected with her work and then only by appointment. "Florence's solitary confinement system" was what one friend called her way of life. The friend used the word "system," because by this time, Nightingale had made the decision to live her secluded, bedridden life on purpose. She felt it was the only way she could guard the time and strength she needed to continue working.

More work than ever

And work she did. Although she now seldom saw government officials personally, she received a constant flow of papers from them. If a British cabinet minister needed expert advice, he contacted Miss Nightingale. If a health official needed a sanitary regulation drafted, he got help from Florence. He knew he would get it back quickly and in a form he could use right away. By now, she was an expert, not only on questions of health and hospitals but on government and legislation as well.

From the quiet of her bedroom, she drew up requests and regulations, drafted proposals for laws, wrote letters, and composed instructions. She had a gift for administration. Long after her death, some of her innovations were still useful. Thirty-seven years after her death, a government investigating committee commented on how well the cost-accounting system of Britain's Army Medical Services, devised in 1861, worked. Other departments had tried much newer methods that failed and were discontinued. They

Florence, grown plump and peaceful. The days of the "Lady With the Lamp" were far in the past. But she still worked for nursing, for the army, for the poor. She was infinitely kind to her nurses, showing them the same concern she had once given to gravely ill governesses she had tended in her youth and to the dying soldiers she had held in the Crimean War.

"Her position was extraordinary. She was, as the men round her delighted to call her, the Commander-in-Chief. She collected the facts, she collated and verified them, she drew the conclusions, she put the conclusions down on paper and finally, she taught them to the men who were her mouthpiece."
Cecil Woodham-Smith, from Florence Nightingale

The conditions in British workhouses were so terrible that people would starve and go without seeing a doctor rather than enter a workhouse.

asked who had thought up the system. The answer? Florence Nightingale.

At forty-one, Nightingale was convinced she had only a few years to live. In fact, she would live to ninety. For at least thirty of these years she continued to be one of the most powerful and respected people in Britain — and the world. She continued her campaigns for reform without any government position or secretarial help — from her sofa or bed!

The British Army in India

In her forties, she turned her attention to another mission that would occupy her for more than thirty years. British soldiers stationed in India were suffering ill health. For years the annual death rate among British soldiers in India had been sixty-nine out of every one thousand. These deaths were caused by unsanitary surroundings and bad water, not war. Some men washed in pie dishes. Sometimes three hundred men slept in one room. Drunkenness was common. Hospital diseases were rampant.

The Indian troops were even worse off. These men had no food, barracks, lavatories, kitchens — nothing. Most other people in India also lived in squalor.

Nightingale realized India needed help. This was a daunting task. She prepared another series of reports, as brilliant as her others. Perhaps the title of a pamphlet she wrote in 1864 says it all: *How people may live and not die in India.*

But nothing had been done in India as 1864 drifted into 1865.

Nightingale could do little without help, but she felt committed to her work. At times, she doubted her usefulness. She often let no one into her room and could tolerate little sound or movement.

She spent thirteen months in her room on a report concerning India and, at last, saw her work bear fruit. The British set up a Sanitary Department in the India Office. It would submit reports on health in India.

By this time, she was forty-seven years old and deeply involved with nursing, Britain's poor, and hospital reform. Her workload was gigantic.

Workhouse reform

She turned her attention now to the problems and dangers poor people faced in Britain's workhouses. In December 1864, a poor man named Timothy Daly had died in Britain's Holborn Workhouse from "filthiness caused by gross neglect." This caused a public outcry, and Florence wrote about the death of Daly to the president of the Poor Law Board. The incident gave her a chance to speak up about how people in workhouses were treated.

In Victorian Britain, the threat of being sent to the workhouse was a nightmare hanging over the lives of the poor. Most Victorians thought that if workhouses were horrible places, people would struggle not to be sent there. But unemployment, bad harvests, illnesses, family tragedies, and old age sent adults and children alike to these institutions, however grim they were. Families were separated. An inmate — for one was a virtual prisoner — felt degraded, like a burden

Workhouses were for the most destitute people. People who were disabled, insane, and orphaned were all kept there in filthy conditions. When poor people became sick, they were sent there. Nightingale spent years campaigning for the reform of these places and for the training of nurses to help in them.

A picture by Sir Luke Fildes of the poor waiting for admission to the charity wards. The notices on the wall are the artist's comment on what crimes these sad, hungry, frozen people would be driven to. Nightingale was to help relieve the plight of these people.

on society. The conditions were often horrible, and only the most sturdy people could survive them.

In 1865, the authorities responded to Florence's efforts. They allowed Nightingale nurses into the Liverpool Workhouse Infirmary on an experimental basis. This was the first time that poor people were cared for by trained staff. The results encouraged everyone, including the authorities. So Nightingale decided to press for an Act of Parliament so that even more wide-ranging workhouse reforms could be made.

First, she said, any workhouse inmates who were physically or mentally ill needed special kinds of care and therefore should have separate institutions. Children, too, had special needs and should have separate institutions with special caretakers. Second, workhouses had to be funded wisely and run according to fair, uniform rules.

In 1867, when Britain's Parliament, after much effort by Nightingale and her supporters, passed the Metropolitan Poor Act, she wrote, "We have obtained some things, the removal of 2,000 lunatics, 80 fever and smallpox cases and all the remaining children out of the workhouses." In addition, there were other reforms. And Nightingale was briefly satisfied, saying, "This is a beginning, we shall get more in time."

Back to St. Thomas's — and her parents

While Florence was working on problems as far away as India and as close as London's workhouses, a problem even closer to her had been festering. In her absence, the Nightingale Training School at St. Thomas's Hospital had fallen away from the high standards she set for it.

In the spring of 1872, she began to investigate the problems at the school. Some reforms and reorganization were vital if the school was to be worthy of its founder's name and reputation. She decided to live close to the hospital and to devote her life to the school and the hospital.

But her plans fell through when she had to concentrate on looking after her aging, ailing parents. During the next few years, she divided her time between caring for them, writing, and working on restoring excellence to the school.

On January 10, 1874, Nightingale received word that her father was dead.

The loss of her father and the full responsibility for her mother, now blind, overwhelmed her. Her life, she wrote, seemed an "utter shipwreck."

But as time passed, she overcame some of her pain. In fact, she enjoyed comparatively quiet years. She worked steadily on. She kept watch over the Nightingale Training School. Her nurses were a constant joy to her. She watched their careers and their successes with great pleasure.

She delighted in the letters that came to her from all over the world. She had achieved so much. The role of women was forever changed. The way people thought of soldiers had changed. Better medical care, better hospitals, better treatment of poor people — in many ways, the wide-ranging reforms in these areas that marked the nineteenth century started with Florence Nightingale. Even so, she never stopped to rest. She was still totally involved, working for new reforms and innovations.

"Do you know what have been the hardest years of my life? Not the Crimean War. Not the 5 years with Sidney Herbert at the War Office when I sometimes worked 22 hours a day, but the last 5 years and three quarters since my father's death."
Florence Nightingale, 1879

Failure and triumph

But in one area, she felt she had failed — India. After another five years or so of detailed work, she wrote in her diary, "Oh that I could do something for India!"

"In 1879," wrote Sir Edward Cook in his 1913 biography, *The Life of Florence Nightingale*, "Miss Nightingale thought that her work as an Indian Reformer had failed."

She had written to every medical officer in India and analyzed their reports. Deaths had fallen drastically as a result of her work. But she felt that her inability to accomplish everything at once meant she had failed.

One of her chief supporters, Sir John Lawrence, the Viceroy of India, died in June 1879. The proposed work was shelved. Reform had failed.

Then on February 2, 1880, her mother died at ninety-two. Florence, at nearly sixty, was free at last.

Somehow, though, those terrible years had healed all the old bitterness. Nursing Fanny and getting to know Parthe better had given Nightingale tolerance and gentleness. The family turned to her when they needed reassurance and advice. Now even her defeats seemed no longer to trouble her as they once had.

But she needn't have felt she was failing. She *was* succeeding, for new reforms were appearing in India.

She was feeling a great deal better, and her life still revolved around her work. She would not see anyone who called without an appointment.

In her lifetime, she had seen revolutionary changes in medicine: anesthesia and modern surgery, Lister's work with antiseptics, and Pasteur's theories about germs and disease.

But none of these discoveries would have had much impact without Nightingale's work in making hospitals places where people went to be cured rather than to die.

Distinguished medical and scientific groups all over the world sought her advice. Even when she was seventy-three, she prepared a lecture that was read at the 1893 World's Columbian Exposition in Chicago. Her store of knowledge, founded on a lifetime of research and experience, was formidable.

Opposite:
Top: Nightingale in old age, serene and beautiful. In her personality she combined two qualities — firmness and kindness. She had always been loved, almost worshipped. Many people have devoted their lives to the ideals that she set before them.

Bottom left: The bedroom where Florence Nightingale spent the last years of her life. She died here when she was ninety.

Bottom right: Claydon House in Buckinghamshire, where Nightingale spent her last years. She came from a world of comfort and dignity. She didn't have to so much as notice the poor and the suffering. But while her later years were sheltered, her mind and heart were with those who suffered.

Old age

Nightingale's old age, in contrast to her stormy and busy life, was happy and peaceful. She was surrounded by people who loved her. The world's rewards often come late, as they did for her.

She kept a close eye on everything, including her own household. It was, of course, immaculate, organized to the last detail. Fresh flowers filled every vase, and the cleanest, crispest linen covered her bed. She interviewed girls who wanted to enter nursing, enjoying their comments.

She and Parthe had put aside their differences. She helped Parthe through her final illnesses, her patience never failing amid pain and difficulty.

After Parthe's death in 1890, Nightingale considered a new idea. What about training health workers who would travel to small towns and teach people basic concepts of hygiene and health? She continued to write letters, "interfering" in the best possible way in matters that concerned her.

Her eyes were failing, but she was in better condition than she had been for years. She was cheerful, and it showed in her plump, mild face, unlike the stern, haggard face of forty years before. She no longer wrote glumly about life. "There is so much to live for," she wrote in 1895. "I have lost much in failures and disappointments, as well as in grief but, do you know, life is more precious to me now in my old age."

A fitting memorial

Gradually, quietly, the tireless Miss Nightingale waned. The mind that had brought so much change to the world began to fade. But the body did not give up easily. By 1901 she could not see at all. But she enjoyed having people read books and newspapers to her daily. And she, in turn, recited famous poems or sang in a voice almost as sweet as it had been in those far-off days in Italy.

Eventually, her mind clouded altogether. By 1906, her household staff had to tell the India Office that there was no longer any point in sending Miss Nightingale papers on sanitary matters.

In November 1907, Britain's King Edward VII

awarded Florence Nightingale the Order of Merit —
the first time this high honor was ever bestowed on a
woman. A representative of the king delivered the
award to her in London, but Nightingale hardly understood what was happening. After murmuring "Too
kind, too kind," Nightingale dropped back to sleep.

She might not have known what the world thought
of her, but the world itself did. Children sent her
birthday cards. Old soldiers who remembered her
wrote to her, sharing their memories.

Then, in 1910, came the fiftieth anniversary of the
Nightingale Training School for Nurses. A meeting at
New York's Carnegie Hall marked the Jubilee. By
then, more than a thousand training schools had been
set up in the United States alone.

Nightingale was unaware of all this. She grew
weaker. On August 13, 1910, at the age of ninety, she
fell asleep and did not wake up.

According to her own wishes, Nightingale was
buried quietly near the family home at Embley.

Only a small cross on the family tombstone marks
her grave. The inscription reads only:

"F. N. Born 1820. Died 1910."

She wanted no other memorial.

Busload after busload of nurses made their way to pay tribute to Florence Nightingale at her funeral in 1910. She had showed herself, beyond doubt, to be one of the most influential, respected people of her time.

For More Information...

Organizations

The organizations listed below can give you more information about Florence Nightingale and other persons devoted to caring for sick people. They can also answer your basic questions about health care issues and about careers in the health professions.

American Assoc. of Nursing Assistants
145 E. 84th Street
New York, NY 10028

American Nurses' Association
2420 Pershing Road
Kansas City, MO 64108

Florence Nightingale Intl. Foundation
3, place Jean Marteau
CH-1201
Geneva, Switzerland

International Health Society
1001 E. Oxford Lane
Cherry Hills Village
Englewood, CO 80110

Natl. Assoc. of Community Health Ctrs.
1330 New Hampshire Ave. NW, Suite 122
Washington, DC 20036

National Council on Alternative
Health Care Policy
P.O. Box 1183
San Jose, CA 95108

National Health Council
622 Third Ave., 34th Floor
New York, NY 10017

National Licensed Practical Nurses
Educational Foundation
P.O. Box 11038
Durham, NC 27703

Books

The following books will give you more information about Florence Nightingale, the nursing profession she devoted her life to, and other subjects related to medicine. Check your local library or bookstore to see if they have them, or ask someone there to order them for you.

About Florence Nightingale —

Florence Nightingale. Hume (Random House)
Florence Nightingale. Peach (Merry Thoughts)
Florence Nightingale. Shor (Silver Burdett)
Florence Nightingale. Turner (Franklin Watts)
Lonely Crusader: The Life of Florence Nightingale 1810-1920. Woodham-Smith
  (Whittlesey House)

About Florence Nightingale and other uncommon people —

Armed with Courage. McNeer and Ward (Abingdon)
Great Women of Medicine. Hume (Random House)

Heroic Nurses. McKown (Putnam)
Hypatia's Sisters: Biographies of Women Scientists, Past and Present. Schacher, ed. (Feminists Northwest)
Lives of Girls Who Became Famous. Bolton (Crowell)
They Changed the World: The Lives of 44 Great Men and Women. Garfinkel (Platt and Munk)
Valiant Women. Pace (Vantage)
Women Who Made History. Borer (Frederick Warne)

About Nursing —

A Day in the Life of an Emergency Room Nurse. Witty (Troll)
Exploring Careers in Nursing. Heron (Rosen Group)
Great Adventures in Nursing. Wright (Harper and Row)
Nurse Power: New Vistas in Nursing. Seide (Lodestar Books)
Nursing. Hodgson (David & Charles)
The Story of Nursing. Dodge (Little, Brown)
Student Nurse: Her Life in Pictures. Engeman (Lothrop, Lee and Shepard)
Women in White. Marks and Beatty (Scribner's)
Your Career in Nursing. Searight (Messner)

Glossary

Almshouse
A place in which poor people lived in earlier times. These houses were either supported through funds given by private individuals and charitable organizations or through taxes. In the United States, almshouses were usually called poorhouses.

Anesthetic
A drug, gas, or similar substance used to deaden pain in a patient. This is usually given before surgery so that the patient loses consciousness.

Annex
A smaller building that is erected near a main building, or an addition attached to the main building.

Barracks
A large building where soldiers live. Now soldiers have beds of their own, with space for storage. In the days of Florence Nightingale, they often needed to share beds because the buildings were crowded. Conditions were unsanitary and therefore unhealthy places for soldiers to live.

Calamity
A terrible misfortune or disaster. A calamity can be caused by humans or by forces in nature.

Campaign
A plan of action. Military personnel and politicians have campaigns, as do many

charitable organizations, businesses, and private individuals who are trying to accomplish some goal.

Cholera
A serious stomach infection, caused by drinking or cooking with polluted water. Its main symptoms are stomach cramps, diarrhea, and vomiting. In Nightingale's time, cholera would kill most of its victims.

Commission, Royal
An official government investigation set up by the queen or king either to find out how laws are working or to examine particular areas of social, educational, or economic concern. A Royal Commission operates within firm guidelines and must make a report to the government stating whether changes must be made and, if so, how they should be made.

Consignment
A shipment of goods. A consignment might include anything from weapons to hospital supplies to farm produce.

Cost-accounting system
A way to keep track of supplies and to estimate how much goods and services are costing an organization.

Crimean War
Fought between 1853 and 1856 by Great Britain, Sardinia, France, and Turkey against the Russian Empire. Russia was trying to expand its territory around the Black Sea at the expense of Turkey. Most of the fighting took place near Varna in what is now Bulgaria and in the Crimean peninsula.

Diplomacy
A tactful and fair way of working with people so that they can retain their pride. Diplomacy demands an understanding of other people and their cultures, as well as of politics.

Dispatch
An official message. Usually, a dispatch is delivered with more speed and urgency than ordinary messages are delivered.

Dysentery
An infection in the intestines. It causes fever, pain, and serious diarrhea.

Gangrene
The decay of the body that occurs when an injury stops the blood from circulating through that part of the body. It is painful and often results in the loss of the body part that is affected.

Hysterics
An attack of uncontrollable laughing or crying, or of a strong emotion, such as

fear or panic. Someone in hysterics might have at least some trouble breathing.

Indefatigable
Tireless, able to keep working for long periods of time.

Infirmary
A place where people who are sick may find care — similar to a hospital but usually not as elaborate and complete in its setup.

Insubordination
Refusing to accept someone's authority. It differs from terms such as *rebellion* in that the insubordinate person will not even recognize authority figures whereas rebellious persons recognize the authority but struggle against it.

Inventory
A list that has been compiled. In the usual sense, one makes an inventory of supplies, but one might also make an inventory of one's blessings, for instance, or an inventory of one's talents.

Larder
A place in which meat and other food is kept, like a pantry or a refrigerator. The larger the number of people to be served, of course, the larger the larder must be.

Memorandum
A note, almost like a letter, that is used as a reminder or a request. A memorandum, called a *memo* for short, is usually sent between people who work in the same company, organization, or building.

Morass
A troublesome situation that is difficult to figure out or get out of. It is named after the kind of marshy, swampy ground that people cannot cross easily — much like a quagmire.

Obituary
A death notice, usually listed in a newspaper, that contains a short retelling of the high points of a person's life.

Pallor
Pale skin tones; having no color; usually associated with illness.

Philanthropist
A wealthy person who is generous with money because of an interest in helping other people or in furthering a cause.

Reprimand
To blame or scold. Often the person who reprimands another is in a position of higher authority.

Scrupulous
Being very careful to do what is morally right, according to one's own principles. Being conscientious about one's beliefs and actions.

Solitary confinement
A condition in which prisoners are kept alone for long periods of time. Sometimes prisoners are put in solitary confinement to break their spirit; at other times they are put there because they are dangerous to guards or to other prisoners.

Squalor
Filth. While we usually use the word to refer to environments, we could also say that a person with few or no principles dwells in moral squalor.

Statistics
A collection of facts and figures about a particular topic that helps you get a mathematical view of the topic. People are often persuaded by statistics when other arguments do not convince them that something is important. Nightingale was brilliant at collecting and remembering facts and figures about health and hospitals, and she was one of the first people in the world to do so.

Subcontinent
A large area of land that is not big enough to be considered a continent. India is a prime example of a subcontinent that is large enough and unique enough to have a personality of its own.

Submissive
Being one who submits to another's authority readily. Being docile, easily led.

Vermin
Any small animal or insect that is a nuisance to humans. Vermin can range from rats and mice that eat and pollute our food to fleas, lice, and other insects that live off human blood. Many vermin carry diseases that they pass on to humans. They are common where conditions are unsanitary.

Victorian
The period of Queen Victoria's rule in Great Britain, 1837-1901; usually associated with many ideas, attitudes, styles, and interests that are generally described by the word "Victorian." Often used in the sense of *prudish* or *narrow-minded*.

Workhouse
In the past, small towns or rural areas had buildings where people who had no money were put to work in return for food and lodging. In Nightingale's day, because people were separated by gender, any family sent to the workhouse was split up. People who were orphaned, insane, or poor and ill were sent to workhouses supported by the local community. They were run cheaply — food was terrible, washing facilities and dormitories were filthy. People avoided workhouses, since they often became sicker than they were at first.

Chronology

1820   **May 12** — Florence Nightingale born in Florence, Italy.

1821   Family returns to Derbyshire, England, where father builds Lea Hurst.

1825   Family moves to Embley Park, near Romsey; establishes routine of summers at Lea Hurst and winters at Embley Park.

1837   **February 7** — Nightingale writes that "God . . . called me to His service" on this day.
September 8 — Starts European tour.

1839   **April** — Nightingale returns to London.

1844   **Spring** — Nightingale recognizes her vocation to be nursing.

1845   **December** — Nightingale announces to her family her plan to enter a nursing career, causing upheaval; begins to study secretly, becoming the first European expert on hospitals and health.

1847   Following a nervous breakdown, Nightingale tours Europe with her friends, Charles and Selina Bracebridge; she meets Liz and Sidney Herbert.

1849   Richard Monckton Milnes proposes marriage to Nightingale; she refuses him for the sake of her vocation, despite her love for him.

1849-50   Nightingale tours Egypt and Greece with the Bracebridges.
Visits the Institution of Deaconesses at Kaiserswerth, Germany.

1851   Returns to study at Kaiserswerth.

1853   Nightingale goes to Paris to train as a nurse.
August 12 — Nightingale becomes Superintendent at London's Institution for the Care of Sick Gentlewomen in Distressed Circumstances.

1854   **March 28** — Britain and France enter the Crimean War as they declare war on Russia.
August — During a cholera epidemic in Britain, Nightingale nurses at the Middlesex Hospital as a volunteer.
September — Allied armies land in the Crimea. Thousands of cholera cases and battle casualties are sent to Scutari.
October 18 — Nightingale appointed by the English Cabinet to be Superintendent of the Female Nursing Establishment of the English General Hospitals in Turkey.
October 21 — Nightingale and thirty-eight of her nurses sail to the Crimea; they arrive November 5.

December — The Army's supply organization has broken down totally. Nightingale is supplying the entire Army's medical service in the Crimea.

1856   **March 30** — Crimean War ends as peace is proclaimed.
July 28 — Nightingale leaves for England with the intention of reforming the Army's medical organization.
September 21 — Nightingale called to meet with Queen Victoria.

1857   Nightingale publishes *Notes on Matters affecting the Health, Efficiency and Hospital Administration of the British Army.*
August — Nightingale collapses and retires as an invalid.

1858   **June** — Nightingale's sister Parthenope marries Sir Harry Verney.
Nightingale writes a pamphlet, *Mortality in the British Army*, which may have been the first pamphlet to use pictorial charts to present statistics.

1859   **Summer** — Nightingale collapses again.
Nightingale's *Notes on Hospitals*, *Notes on Nursing*, and *Suggestions for Thought* published.

1860   **June 24** — Nightingale Training School opens in St. Thomas's Hospital.

1861   **April** — Civil War starts in United States; Nightingale later asked to organize hospitals and the care of the sick and wounded.
August 2 — Sidney Herbert dies.
Nightingale's *Notes on Nursing for the Labouring Classes* is published.
December — Again Nightingale collapses. She is bedridden for six years.

1862   Her *Observations by Miss Nightingale*, in the Indian Sanitary Commission's Report, inspires a sanitary reform movement in India.

1864   **January** — Nightingale writes *Suggestions in regard to Sanitary Works Required for the Improvement of Indian Stations.*

1865   **October** — Nightingale moves to No. 35 South St., London, later to be known as No. 10, where she lives for the rest of her life.

1867   **June** — Nightingale starts collecting statistics on deaths in childbirth. This takes three years.
October — She is asked to write a study of Indian sanitary questions.
December — Florence collapses from overwork. Afterward she finds it difficult to concentrate.

1868   Nightingale writes "Una and the Lion," about Nightingale nurses working at the Liverpool Workhouse Infirmary.

1870   British Red Cross Aid Society founded.

1872	International Committee of the Red Cross founder Henry Dunant claims that Nightingale's work in the Crimea influenced his ideas. Nightingale feels she must help her parents, who can no longer cope with running their two houses.
1874	**January** — Father dies. Nightingale publishes a pamphlet, *Suggestions for Improving the Nursing Service for the Sick Poor*.
1877	Famine in India; four million die.
1880	**February 2** — Mother dies.
1883	Sister Parthe is seriously ill; Florence takes charge.
1887	Queen Victoria celebrates fifty years of her reign with a Jubilee — in the fiftieth anniversary year of Nightingale's first "call." British Nurses' Association organized.
1890	Nightingale's sister Parthe dies.
1896	Nightingale again confined to her bedroom — this time, permanently.
1897	A famous bust of Nightingale and the carriage she used in the Crimea are displayed in an exhibit on the progress of trained nursing at the Victorian Era Exhibition, part of Queen Victoria's Diamond Jubilee.
1901	Nightingale becomes blind.
1907	**November** — Britain's King Edward VII bestows the Order of Merit on Nightingale; it is the first time that the Order is given to a woman.
1908	Freedom of the City of London awarded to Nightingale.
1910	**August 13** — Nightingale dies in her sleep.
1915	A statue of Florence Nightingale is erected at the Crimea Memorial, Waterloo Place, London.

Index